Revolution

MaryAnn Hayatian

ButterflyAnthology

www.butterflyanthology.com

family
understanding is already a complete
ambition of inspiration and acceptance

Poetry

Revolution

The society is mending

Its cruel character

Of shallowness.

Acceptance is to progress.

The sun has stayed

Everlasting.

People won't look at you

As an outsider

Those are the ones

That need guidance.

Home

A comfort spot with warm thought

No poison to destroy your feelings

Nobody telling you to do so

No pressure and stress

No one to decrease your self esteem

And joke on your goals

A smile and being with you

Is home

Wellness

Heal yourself

Inspire to create

Viral people disappear on your permission

Grow your garden

understand your condition

Medication pretends

Aware the health

Energy sends

Guardian

Receiving is an award from your support.

Weakness is the creation to strong ability.

Defence fragility is the silver flower once it's under your protection.

An angel functions your human self from the tranquility

Vision pursue for us to be careful.

Hypocrisy

A masked serpent

Slides near your way

With a nice and unknown feature

On it's face

Getting its power by it

While it acts a counterfeit personality.

It slides back to deteriorate you

Without a trace.

As you are a person of kindness

And you are the person of distress.

By a serpent from a senseless circus of greed

Who knows how to play.

Its speech is meaningless

What is left are crumbs

Of scars

Dissolving with a coated silence.

Human

We were not born as models

With a perfect body.

As we grow

We change

And value the importance

Of a person's character.

Not a person's figure.

Media

A glare of one's reflection

Has been a topic of nothing.

Its goal is bought by its being

Spending waste less fortune for attention.

Television is taught for gossip

Not education.

The unknowledged has time to pertain

The destruction of this has nothing to gain.

All is entertainment

For the society

Their so called fame.

Delusion

Hypnotized by its own make belief land

Consuming anything

With your command.

The idea is one way to follow

Even if you're wrong

The colors are still to your direction.

No sense of gravity

Around the people surrounding you

No thoughts of what they are going through.

A person like this is described as a cartoon.

Ridicule opportunity

The impatient stand by to leave

A place of misery

And

Arrive to a better location.

It's a place for options.

Though some depreciate the nation land

Your rules our brought with your head

Disturbing others

While contemporary locals reside and work

On their goals

For light

Nothing is free.

You cannot control and disappoint

This country of prospect

With what you brought

Under your sleeve.

This is not entitled an autocracy

It's a place for a stream of variety.

Arrogance

This can stop

No not with your money

No not with your pity.

Swallow your shallowness

Your know it all tune

And

Accept what people are.

Why don't you use some sagacity

Than destroying others.

You make a war out of nothing

There won't be an audience to participate

Your show.

Last laugh

It's daft how you can joke

About a person's talent

Because you have nothing else to do

Increasing around your games to people

And shredding its art.

Where is the support from the other artist?

As you claim to be.

Where is your professionalism?

If you want to make it after

Your amateur analysis.

Lousy and lame

Your title defines shame.

A blank and stranded thing

You are known as the society discloses.

Go play

Where people will laugh at you with content.

There's nothing resourceful with your work

Just a prototype of agony.

Profligate

There are matters

To whom it may concern

How to survive

And

Why

Do they exist

These people

That don't define cheerfulness.

How can people stand still

When our world is always changing

As they are in front of the sun

Devoid of a conclusion.

And

Keep away from the dark shade of pretending.

Cruel world

Judged by the amount of education

Not the eminence of knowledge

Friends with two faces

Have been a ravage in most cases.

Materials are significant

Being poor have been mistreated.

Categorized as a label

Of an indefinite

Don't mislead

Don't be superficial

Don't interfere

Agree whom an individual is

And

Mind your own business

Autumn

The crisp colorful view

Draws on a light day

Like a sketch.

The dew in the morning

Stays frosted like cereal

And

As soggy like milk when it rains.

First snow

Symbol of the holidays

Are approaching

Quiet as the flakes appearing

Colored lights shine

As they bring people together

Warming up on this cold weather

Last day of winter

The snow has covered the earth

Watching from the window

A black and white slide show.

A rainbow sprinkles its colors

And melts the icy shadow.

You start to see

the vision of the sky

Liberate you

From the melancholy.

Spring revelry

The green is the scene

And

Beings are the art

Of a painting.

Conversate in a group

With tea and little things

Made out of sugar.

A corner of dancing

As they observe their parading.

It continues as it dawns

And

Lanterns keep the crowd bright.

Summer orchard

The warm air swirls

Around with a scent

Of wood fire and apples

Upon the area of harvest

And

the shore reflecting its waves

From the glare

Of the cabins' glassed doors.

Magical garden

Strolling amongst in the fields

Where strings of flowers

Direct to an alley

Of Imagination.

Figures of fireflies

Showing you the way

To the ponds

And

The crystal streams

Of essence.

Architecture

Decades pass

As the still foundation of edifices remain

As it is.

People reside and depart

And the structures define

History.

All denote a story

Of a once upon a time,

And

An accolade of hard work and achievement

Set by a person for its gratitude

Elixir

Perseverance is prescribed everyday
It helps to maintain the goals
You are achieving for.
Your indications recommence
By a supremacy
Of your dynamism.

Celebrity

Spotlight of Hollywood
Attentive to watchers
All the glam and money
Will take you to the top
Stepping to high grounds
Is not a definition
To overdose
Fans are mentored
By you
Not how much you make
You inspire them
On creating
Not pursuing a drug intake
As a star
You are responsible
To prevent
Young ones
Want to be
Just like you
There is no reason
To suffer
Your image

Shouldn't be a result
Of mislead

Facade

As fragile and kind the society can be

There's no consideration

Just brutal despondently

Among a soundless reply.

From those who are in a centric sphere

Walking in the air

And

Think only of themselves.

They are act and cloth differently in any location

Like at a party

With a finale

An illustration of ugliness

They are nothing.

No logic, but a disrupt of sentences

Disfiguring a dialogue

A decadence.

Authenticity

You are true

Without a uniform

Sculpted your ordinary aptitude

And

Munificent to humanity.

Not a subjective for notice

A leader

Not programmed

By a broken record.

You have your own mind to speak

You're not weak.